ABOUT *TRAVEL FOR SENIORS MADE EASY*

"For nearly twenty years, the Eichers have been clients and dear personal friends. During that time, I have sent them on trips throughout the world. They are discerning travelers who have a clear vision of what they need, desire, and hope for, as far as traveling is concerned. They travel within their physical limitations, yet through excellent planning, they have wonderful adventures. I accompanied them on a trip that they were leading for 30 members of their church—from Berlin to Prague, cruising the Elbe River in what was formerly East Germany. The trip retraced the life and ministry of Martin Luther, not a favorite of mine as a Roman Catholic! Nevertheless, the trip was fun, memorable and educational, as I enjoyed seeing the historical sites and meeting many wonderful people."

—Rose Marie Maher, Owner
The Carefree Traveler
Carefree, Arizona

TRAVEL FOR
SENIORS
MADE *EASY*

STAYING **ALIVE** @ 65

TRAVEL FOR
SENIORS
MADE *EASY*

STAYING **ALIVE** @ 65

250 plus International Sites Visited and
Recommended as Senior Friendly

More Than 120 Solid Pieces of Travel Advice

Over 35 Personal Travel Anecdotes!

MIKE **EICHER**

TATE PUBLISHING
AND ENTERPRISES, LLC

Published by Tate Publishing & Enterprises, LLC
127 E. Trade Center Terrace | Mustang, Oklahoma 73064 USA
1.888.361.9473 | www.tatepublishing.com

Tate Publishing is committed to excellence in the publishing industry. The company reflects the philosophy established by the founders, based on Psalm 68:11,
"The Lord gave the word and great was the company of those who published it."

Book design copyright © 2013 by Tate Publishing, LLC. All rights reserved.
Cover design by Rodrigo Adolfo
Interior design by Jake Muelle

Published in the United States of America

ISBN: 978-1-62510-519-6
1. Travel / Special Interest / Senior
2. Travel / Genera
13.05.14

Eichers at Geiranger Fjord, Norway

DEDICATION

Dedicated to my wife, Lassie, and daughters, Ardith and Tiscia, my lifetime travel companions

Lassie, Tiscia, Mike, and Ardith Eicher
at Victoria Falls in Africa

ACKNOWLEDGEMENTS

Often a book is loaded with acknowledgements, professionals or friends who conducted research, tracked down little-known or remembered facts, etc. In my case, this has been a family affair. I am deeply indebted to my daughters, one in Santa Fe and the other in Chicago, who have provided photos, layout advice, and remembrances—all while conducting their own very busy lives. My wife, editor, and traveling companion has been particularly helpful in assuring that my humor will come through, without destroying the accuracy of the content. I must admit that I have not checked to see that every one of my assertions is still true—but I do believe that the Trevi Fountain still exists in Rome, although I haven't personally seen it for a few years. Most of the book is my own expressed opinion—I've "researched my mind" to bring that forward. My wife's journals and camera recorded the information that brought our recollections into focus.

I also am indebted to several friends who provided advice on how to get this book published—a daunting task for a novice author.

TABLE OF CONTENTS

PREFACE

This book is written as a guide for all of the seniors who could still be traveling, but have decided that it is too much trouble, now that they are sixty-five or over. The need to write this book came to me in the dining room of our continuing care retirement community, listening to a multitude of fellow residents tell me how very much they used to enjoy travel, but now it is too much hassle. Also, it is written for the millions of baby boomers, now retiring, who may not have had much opportunity to travel when they were working.

Most of these seniors loved traveling when they were younger—on business or on vacation, with their spouse and family. Traveling took them throughout the world; they covered all continents and the high seas.

For me, travel and the love of adventure began when I was a young boy and accompanied my parents during summer vacations. During the 1950s, we crisscrossed the United States and Canada. I also traveled to Europe as an exchange student and visited Cuba with my great-aunt. All of this travel was done somewhat on an economy budget, but enjoyable nonetheless.

After college, my wife and I were stationed in Hawaii, courtesy of the US Navy. During our three-year tour, we managed to visit most of the Hawaiian Islands and I was fortunate enough to make a side trip to American Samoa.

During our thirty-seven year career in the corporate world, business and pleasure took my wife and me, as well as our two daughters, to Europe several times, to Japan, Hong Kong, Singapore, Malaysia, Australia, Indonesia, New Zealand, Philippines, Borneo, Tahiti, and to many of the islands in the Caribbean. Many of these trips we planned ourselves, preferring to set our own pace and itinerary rather than being a part of a tour. When we traveled without the children, we often had no advance reservations or preconceived notions of the sights we might be seeing. We always ate well, saw the important landmarks, and planned time for wandering.

Touring the cities of the world via self-guided walking tours was always a great way to spend a day— Paris, London, Rome, Munich, Sydney, Auckland, Athens, Istanbul, Bangkok, and Kuala Lumpur, just to name a few. It helped us to understand how different yet the same the peoples of the world could be. Language, currency, dress, customs, culture and song provided vibrant evidence of peoples' similarities.

Exposure to the great art and architecture, literature and the music of distant lands gives you, and especially your children, an appreciation of life that can never be found in books or in films. Travel builds tolerance, understanding, and an appreciation of things different from what one finds at home. We always said when a trip would require the children to miss school, "Let not school stand in the way of our children's education." Our tall blond daughters with straight hair to their waists being stared at like Hollywood stars on the Tokyo subway, my wife having to eat chicken soup with the head and feet of the chicken still attached at a business dinner in Taipei, my being banned for life from German youth hostels (missed curfew)—these incidents have added fabric to our lives and have enriched us.

Looking at photo albums, digital photos, 35 mm slides, and recalling various trips and sights with the family over the years have brought back fabulous memories that we love sharing with the kids during our family times together. It breaks our hearts to hear other seniors, like ourselves, say that those things are all things of the past. They don't have to be—this book is a guide to traveling as seniors just as enjoyably, but somewhat differently. Of course, we are all different in terms of physical conditioning, temperament, stamina, etc., and those things must be taken into consideration.

Since retiring, we have visited Montreal, Quebec City, Halifax, London, Edinburgh, Vancouver, Anchorage,

Copenhagen, Dublin, Amsterdam, Cologne, Frankfort, Vienna, Budapest, Stockholm, Johannesburg, Cape Town, Helsinki, St. Petersburg, Tallinn, Berlin, Bordeaux, Paris, Lisbon, Seville, Granada, Malaga, Barcelona, Monte Carlo, Nice, Oslo, Bergen, Cartagena, Panama City, Santiago, Montevideo, Venice, Florence, Pisa, Rome, Casablanca, Rio de Janeiro, Gibraltar, Tangier, Lima, Acapulco, Osaka, Seoul, Dresden, Mainz, Vienna, Geneva, Zurich, Bratislava, and Buenos Aires, as well as the islands of Sicily, Corsica, Majorca, Roatan and the Caymans. Our itineraries have also included Costa Rica, Mexico, Belize, and Honduras. This represents quite a bit of travel since we became seniors, and we have loved every minute of it; though, admittedly, it has become a "different kind" of travel than the trips that we made in earlier decades.

Okay, let's get started. How do old, frail codgers manage to have wonderful travels?

WHY TRAVEL AT ALL AS SENIORS?

Travel is stimulating activity! Seeing new things, going to new places—these are the kinds of things that help keep your brain active and alert as you age. The experience of traveling makes you a more interesting conversationalist at the dinner table and at parties. Travel adds meaning and patina to your life. Travel will reduce the number of items on your bucket list.

Before we travel, we must make a serious and realistic assessment of our ability, both mental and physical, to undertake traveling. At our age, if it isn't fun, why do it? Your self-assessment will dictate the type of travel that will suit you. We all are at different places on the physical/stamina scale.

In my own case, though I walk with the aid of a cane for balance, I can get along pretty well unless climbing stairs, long walks, altitude, and extremely hot/humid conditions are issues (unless I can find a place to sit for a few minutes). Others my age have no troubles at all with ambulation, while another group may need walkers or wheelchairs to move from place to place. Still others may have different medical limitations, such as high blood pressure, altitude sickness, heart problems, etc.

None of these limitations should preclude one from traveling but should guide their choices of transport and destination venues. One must think not only of his/her physical limitations, but about minimizing tension and stress; both can be exhausting and can spoil the trip. Group travel need not be excluded; there are high-end travel group tour leaders that are most accommodating, if this type of travel is your preference. The only significant barrier that I can foresee would be the inability to climb on and off a motor coach without major assistance. Otherwise, I've found tour leaders, ship personnel, and employees of other modes of transportation most accommodating.

Another stimulus of travel is the fun and excitement of learning about where you will be going ahead of time. Reading books, maps, looking at movies and pictures all add immensely to the travel experience for me. The in-depth anticipation provided by advance preparation is often almost as much fun as the travel itself. Also, by reviewing what each day's itinerary holds for you, you can determine in advance whether or not you will be up to that day's challenge. It's important to leave yourself an "out option" for uncertain activities that can be decided at the last minute—stay aboard the ship, stay aboard the bus, "wait 'here' until the group returns to me." Thinking about this, some wonderful venues come to mind that make a senior's experience as good as anyone's.

I have often had wonderful experiences talking with the locals while my group has gone on ahead to see a sight and I decided to hang out by the bus and await their return—often talking to the bus driver!

IT COSTS MONEY TO BE A SPORT

This book is about senior travel made easy—I never said that it would be inexpensive! When we lose mobility, agility, and the desire to explore the unknown on our own and at our own pace, the trade-off for structure and ease of travel is the simple fact that it costs more. I choose to look at the costs this way: one-third will be paid by the government (income taxes), one-third will be paid by my children (inheritance), so that leaves only one-third for me to pay! When you look at it that way, it is not too bad.

> We've always told the kids that we plan to spend it all, only saving enough at the end for a new Cadillac to sit in with the motor running in an enclosed garage. When I asked our older daughter what she thought of that, she said, "Dad, that depends. What color is the Cadillac?"

My father always said "It costs money to be a sport" when the family was considering a special outing that cost a bit more than usual. Let's review these "extra" costs again.

First, you would need transportation to the airport in a private car service (not a taxi). Second, you would request a curbside wheelchair to get you and your spouse checked in, through security, and delivered to your gate. You want a wheelchair reserved at your destination as well. Third, you will want business-class airfare and private transportation to take you from your destination airport to your hotel or directly to the ship. These aforementioned "extras" apply regardless of your ultimate destination.

Assuming that you are going on a cruise, additional extras are involved. You may want a stateroom with a veranda, especially useful if you expect sunny, comfortable weather, and a location that will entitle you to concierge service. All other costs would be the same regardless of your age or ambulation.

When you arrive home, after one of life's more wonderful trips, you will find that the extras you spent would have bought you only a couple more weeks in the nursing home someday! If you spend the children's inheritance on the children (invite them along), it will be a happier day for them when your last will is being read.

DECIDE TO TAKE UP TRAVEL AGAIN

L et us think about some of the preliminary factors that will help us decide whether or not we are up to resuming travel.

SET PARAMETERS

First, one must deal with their own mind-set. Do you still want to see and do new things or visit old favorites (which may be easier)? Do you have someone with whom to share new experiences, someone who is compatible as a traveling companion, a good friend or a family member? We do not recommend traveling alone; companionship is important for your sense of well-being. At our age, medical problems or accidental falls are a real possibility. Are foreign experiences still stimulating and enriching? Are you more comfortable staying in the United States? If you are ready to get back to some traveling, it's time to get started.

There are various methods of travel that appeal to and are safe for seniors. We think for many reasons the best type of travel for seniors may be *cruising*. This can be ocean cruising or river cruising. Cruising provides structure—your cabin is set, mealtimes are set, and the itinerary is set. You unpack one time and bring your "hotel" along with you. Fellow cruisers can be engaged or ignored as you wish.

No one our age should need to deal with packing and unpacking, embarking and disembarking the buses, trains, and taxis multiple times during the day. Those are among the things that make travel miserable and exhausting! While cruising may appear front and center in this book, it is not recommended for or desired by everybody. We highlight it because of the expense involved and the fact that there are many decisions to be made in cruising—it's not like booking a flight, hotel room, and rental car!

> Once, when booking a rental car in Germany, we neglected to ask how to open the gas cap on the rental Mercedes. At an autobahn service station, when needing to fill the tank, we were in a jam, until a German lady who spoke excellent English, came to our rescue! We also found, in England, that driving on the opposite side from the American way could be very disconcerting.

USE REFERENCES, INTERNET, AND SOCIAL NETWORKS

Referring again to travel preparation, we seniors tend to buy books, maps, and watch TV to get ready. The Travel and Discovery channels, Fodor's and Frommer's travel guides, *National Geographic* magazine, Rick Steves's guides/ travelogues, and the *World Atlas* are usually my resource materials for travel preparation. I also read the travel section of our Sunday newspaper, and subscribe to *Travel + Leisure* as well as *Conde Nast Traveler*. I would recommend these two magazines to anyone with the slightest interest in travel. The information is accurate and very well presented. Most book stores have excellent travel sections/departments.

Today, social media (Facebook and Twitter) can provide up-to-the-minute info on travel from people who are on the scene in real time. The internet search engines (Google and Yahoo!) can instantly bring you information and maps for anywhere you plan to go. If you are uncomfortable about using the internet, have your grandchildren look up stuff. You'll all get educated together!

TRAVEL WITH OTHERS

Many people prefer cruising with friends. I find that the best friends are "family." Specifically, I am talking about adult children. I recommend *one child per cruise*, with you paying the cruise fare. The child should have the wherewithal to handle his/her own airfare. Married children, without their spouse and kids, are as much candidates to join you as single children. You may not have had extended one-on-one time with this child for over fifty years! They really enjoy traveling with you, and they make wonderful luggage handlers! You can rely on them to take their turn as "day chairman." They don't have to do everything you do, including shore excursions, but they will plan the dining venues and other onboard activities.

> We recently took a cruise to Central America with our older daughter. She appreciated a little "break" from her family and a chance to travel to a region she hadn't been to before. We appreciated her assistance. Some days, we all shared the same shore excursion—air boating in Belize for example; other days, my wife and I did one thing while our daughter chose something else. (We passed on the all-terrain vehicles in Cozumel!) That flexibility is just one of the beauties of cruising. But we always met up for dinner to recount our adventures, and we made a more diverse team for the nightly trivia contest!

Even when traveling with good nonfamily friends, it is tiring saying "What do you want to do?" and getting replied by "What do you want to do?" every day. It seems to work well that the choice of excursions is each individual's choice each day. Then the group gets together in the evening for cocktails and dinner arranged by the person designated as "day chairman" for that day (which rotates daily).

The downside of such travel in a group is that you hardly ever meet new folks.

AVOID LONG WALKS AND LONG LINES

If seventy-plus, it is a good idea to invest less than twenty dollars at your neighborhood pharmacy and purchase a walking cane. A cane adds safety and steadying on unfamiliar surfaces like cobblestones, and also, it is good for "early boarding" on airplanes, as well as ships, for you as well as your companion. We are not talking about "pretending" to be handicapped to gain some advantage when you are not; nevertheless, at our age, protecting against falling is most legitimate! Others are respectful of a person with a cane; they will let you pass and give you your space. A walking cane should be placed in the hand *opposite your weaker leg*.

The four most powerful words a senior can utter when at the airport are, "I'll need a wheelchair." Don't be too proud or think that you are too able to make this request. It saves a huge amount of time, stress, exhaustion, and pain from long walks and waits.

> A dear friend was told by us to request a wheelchair at the airport on a recent trip to Geneva, Switzerland. Reluctantly, he did so, and he later told us that it was the best travel advice that he had ever received!

A wheelchair engaged at curbside will give you expedited treatment when checking luggage, checking in, waiting passport control and, most importantly, moving through security. Retaining the skycap pusher until you are delivered to the gate can easily save you an hour and reduce exhaustion, at a busy airport during heavy travel times. With the skycap pusher, you can stop for a snack or a newspaper or to use the bathroom. From the curb to the gate, this is a service worth at least a twenty-dollar tip. Your spouse will benefit too; all carry-on bags can be placed on your lap for the ride through the airport. For those who need a wheelchair throughout their trip, we recommend checking WheelchairTraveling.com.

The evidence of a cane or walker will usually get you "early boarding" on the ship as well—even though you haven't paid for it. No escaping the life-boat drill, however! I have always found ship's crew and agents handling shore excursions to be most sensitive and accommodating—and willing to go the extra mile for those demonstrating a need for some assistance.

FIND A TRAVEL AGENT

We are past (too old) the point in time where it is fun to plan a detailed itinerary on our own. You may have used a travel agent in the past from whom you purchased airline tickets or through whom you booked hotel rooms. If this agent is knowledgeable, trustworthy, and knows something about the cruising- , resort-, or destination-event industries, you have probably found a winner!

Now is the time to spill the beans regarding your likes and dislikes. Where would you like to go, how long are you willing to be gone, and how many fellow travelers can you tolerate? Do you prefer a single big event (Olympics, Wimbledon, World Cup, the Kentucky Derby, for example), or would you be more comfortable having a headquarters (a ship or resort) and branching out on excursions from there or just sitting quietly reading a great novel at a luxurious destination?

Ship size, the crew-to-guest ratio, country of registry, year that the ship first sailed, type and variety of cuisine, cabin size, shore excursions offered, entertainment, casino, health spa and fitness facilities are all important amenities about which most cruisers feel quite strongly.

Having now "bonded" with your travel agent, you are ready to discuss the pros and cons of various ships, their itineraries, and the pricing of the cruise or other types of trips. Once the basics have been settled, it is time to sweat the details, or better yet, tell your travel agent to sweat the details. Cruises are now about the only phase of travel where the travel agent still gets a sizeable percentage of the booking as a commission. Therefore, the agent should be willing to devote sufficient time to your wishes and desires for you to enjoy complete satisfaction.

PACK THE ESSENTIALS

The first two questions relating to packing: where are we going and what time of year will it be when we arrive? Next, will there be a special event that dictates certain dress? If on a cruise ship, is the policy of the cruise line formal or country-club casual?

Now you are ready to begin. We will keep in mind weight, bulk, and flexibility. The cardinal rule: pack as little as possible. Whatever you have put out on the bed, put one-half of it back in the closet prior to opening the suitcase. By the way, lightweight suitcases with pull-up handles and rollers are recommended.

> Plan for luggage emergencies: Always pack a change of clothes in your carry-on bag, in case your luggage is delayed. Also, traveling partners should place one outfit in each other's suitcase in case one suitcase takes a *scenic route* to your destination!

Have ID attached to each bag and put a copy of it *inside* the bag.

Guys should always take the obligatory blue blazer for warmth and in case the ship's radio officer invites you to dinner! Shoes should be kept to a minimum, one pair for daytime (walking) and a pair for evening wear. Shoes are both heavy, and they take up a lot of room. Two pair of slacks should do it, one khaki and one dark in color. Collared sport shirts and a few polo shirts to go along with two pair of bermuda shorts swimming trunks, and you guys are set.

One controversial category: underwear. It's rather bulky, so you can't pack enough for a long cruise, and you don't want to do much laundry. Consider going "commando" for a week or two. It won't kill you, and you might get a kick out of it! I won't presume to tell women what to pack; they know instinctively, but they still pack too much. The keys are: few shoes and mix-and-match layered clothing.

My wife insisted that the following be added: Gals, you should use a single basic color scheme— *black, blue, or brown,* so you can mix, match, and layer. Then you only need a daytime pair and a dress pair of shoes in that one basic color. Colorful scarves are magical for converting one outfit into many. Avoid anything that wrinkles or is not comfortable. Remember, one suitcase per person maximum, so less is more! Include something that will be conservative and appropriate when visiting cathedrals, shrines, cemeteries, etc.

Clothing is not the most important packing ingredient for seniors—spare equipment, medicines, and toiletries are. Spare eyeglasses, prescription sunglasses, teeth, hearing aids (batteries), plus prescription medications are critical. Medicines should be packed in the "daily compartments" and should always be taken in the hand luggage/carry-on of yourself and your spouse. *Never* pack medicine or valuables in checked luggage. If certain medicine is critical to life support (insulin, heart, altitude, blood pressure, etc.), take more than you will need to account for any unplanned delay. The good news is that ship dispensaries carry the most common prescriptions and will cover you in an emergency. It is a good idea to carry copies of your written prescriptions in case of Customs or Security inquiries.

I ran out of Procardia (blood pressure) medicine once, but the nurse in the dispensary was happy to give me a few pills—no questions asked.

I mention toiletries only because seniors are used to certain brands and are comfortable with their own stuff. There will be toiletries in your cabin, but you may not like them or they could cause an allergic reaction. Seniors particularly like their own hair dryer! Find space to fit it in. Guys, if you are lucky enough to still have hair, you'll be glad that you did.

My second cardinal rule of packing: pack equipment and medicines *first* in your carry-on bag—regardless of where you are going and your mode of transportation. Then pack the suitcase with toiletries and clothing.

Something to consider wearing, not packing, is a lightweight, reversible, fleece/water-resistant jacket. Put a pair of gloves and a scarf in the pockets; you will be glad you did, as the weather can change quickly! Also recommended for seniors is wearing compression stockings during any long flight—it helps circulation.

❑ **Luggage**

Always check your luggage (big or small), and use a skycap whenever possible. This will increase your level of comfort when moving through airports, changing planes, waiting at gates or passenger lounges. One fairly large carry-on bag that fits under the seat or in the overhead bin is all you will need with you. It should have several zippered pockets and be large enough to accommodate your tickets, money, jewelry, passports, itinerary, insurance policy, camera, cell phone, and medicines. Speaking of cell phones, you will need adaptors and transformers in order to use the electrical appliances, *chargers, dryer, razor, etc.* The appliances will be useless without the exact adaptors and transformers needed for each country visited, although many ships have plugs for 120V wiring.

❑ **Laundry**

Whether in a hotel or aboard ship, take advantage of the laundry services available. Yes, they are expensive, but your vacation time is more valuable doing almost anything else, but laundry. In the Laundromats aboard ship, you will see passengers sitting, waiting for the washer or dryer when they could be out enjoying sightseeing in places that they will never see again.

METHODS OF TRAVEL OTHER THAN OCEAN LINERS

An important key for successful travel for Seniors is to minimize the need for packing and unpacking, as well as the number of times the luggage must be handled. Here are some alternatives other than travel on large cruise ships that can be equally enjoyable.

RIVER CRUISING

We have had delightful river cruises throughout Europe: on the Rhine, Elbe, Seine, Danube, and Main rivers. Cabins are smaller, amenities fewer, cuisine not so fancy, but wholesome and lots of fun nevertheless. Be sure to book your stateroom on an upper floor—the lowest level can often look out on the algae-covered wall of a pier rather than at the scenery when docked.

Ocean and river cruising are two entirely different ballgames, but in general, the same rules apply. You are never bored on a river cruise because the shoreline is just a short distance away and the scenery is always changing. River cruising is usually a bit less expensive, and the shore excursions may involve a bit more challenge as you dock near a city center and walk into town. Also, excursions are often made at no additional charge. The boat moves quite slowly—we did a seven-day Seine River cruise from Paris to the battlefields of Normandy. The return from Le Havre to the Paris airport took only one and a half hours by motor coach!

If castles, cathedrals, and enjoying the beautiful European countryside are your thing, then by all means, consider a river cruise. While we have never traveled the rivers of China or Russia, we hear that they are fabulous.

> While cruising on the Main in Germany, we had a gentleman come aboard who conducted a glass-blowing demonstration. When we docked the next morning in Wertheim, he was there to meet us and escort us to his shop. Needless to say, he enjoyed excellent sales that morning! Those making special presentations and entertainers can come aboard and get off at the next port, ensuring excellent quality resources.

DESTINATION TRAVELS

There are those who prefer to go to one place and "park it" as opposed to being in motion every night. This is especially true if traveling involves attending some big event upon arrival. We do recommend this type of travel for seniors because the continual packing-unpacking, transferring of luggage, and climbing on and off motor coaches are exhausting.

Destination travel, most assuredly, requires the involvement of a professional, trustworthy travel agent. If you want to go to England to see Wimbledon, it is disastrous to arrive and find that you have no tennis tickets or that the ones you do have are fakes or for the wrong day! (Remember, no refunds and no exchanges.)

This becomes more important wherever the crowds will be larger and the event(s) more popular. For example, the Olympics (summer or winter games) come to mind. Our best advice here: *do not leave home without every phase of your travels confirmed and in hand.*

Your flights, hotel accommodations, transfers, and event tickets *must be* in your possession and include evidence that you have prepaid, if such is the case. Your passport, visa (if required), and proof of travel insurance need to be with you as well. There is nothing worse than discovering that your tickets are for a different day and that they are not exchangeable when you are standing in front of the venue six thousand miles from home and the travel agent!

Also, a word of caution—although there is nothing that you can do about it—there is no such thing as a rain check at Wimbledon. Why? *Because all days are sold out!* If it rains on your day, such is life! Go back to your hotel or visit some other attraction.

When a famous museum is included on a particular shore excursion, it is usually possible to obtain your entrance ticket ahead of time, thus avoiding long lines by entering through a separate door.

If you are exploring a city on your own, purchase multiple tickets to various venues from your hotel concierge, again avoiding long entrance lines. If a city is new to you, the Gray Line, or equivalent, city highlight tour is valuable as you get your bearings. Always try to book an English Only tour, and if possible, avoid the height of the local tourist season.

> Even the best laid plans can go awry. We recently planned a third cruise to Alaska for later this summer. (Being from Arizona, we can't get enough of Alaska in the summertime). Anyway, the ship deposit, insurance, and airfare had all been paid. We came to find out that the cruise was to be in 2013, not 2012, although it was listed in the 2012 catalogue! Our travel agent had missed it as well. We are now in the process of collecting refunds and rebooking. Better our travel agent do it than attempting it ourselves. Because we have had a twenty-year relationship with our agent, I'm sure that it will all work out.

AFFINITY TRIPS

Traveling with like-minded people can be very comforting for some, even giving up a bit of comfort in exchange for the companionship of those with similar likes and interests. In particular, I'm thinking of university-sponsored trips or those arranged by your club, interest group, residence, or place of worship.

> We took a family trip, which was university sponsored, to South Africa, where we stayed at the Thornybush Game Reserve at the edge of Kruger National Park. Although we were in the "bush," our accommodations were "first class" and we did see the Big Five from the comfort of our Land Rover and with the expert commentary of our driver and "tracker." This was an outstanding family vacation, and we ran into a fraternity brother we knew from school. Another fellow about our age on the trip noticed our daughter's unusual name and said that he was in love with a girl by that name back in college. We realized that our daughter was actually named after his college girlfriend whom we knew there too!
>
> We also led a church tour on an Elbe River cruise that traced the life and ministry of Martin Luther. Having communion in the cathedral in Wittenberg, Germany, where Luther tacked up *The Ninety-Five Theses* on the door was very special as the sacraments were given by our own pastor.
>
> On affinity trips, we have ended up traveling with many friends of friends.

Our Cornell University group on safari in South Africa.

ELDERHOSTEL

This travel approach is like an affinity trip—like-minded travelers in search of deeper knowledge about a place or concept. Elderhostel has been around for many years. Originally, older people were housed in spartan (hostel) accommodations. Over time, the clientele changed and superior accommodations were requested regularly. Now the participants stay in "nice" accommodations, and the name is being changed to Road Scholars. You can reach them online and request that you be sent a complete catalogue.

ANCESTRY-SEARCH ("ROOTS") TRIP

Many seniors find that this time of life is the perfect time to trace their roots or ancestry. For many, this search finds its way to places other than the United States. Genealogical records are now available via many sources, including Ancestry.com on the Internet. To visit family homesteads and meet distant relatives, visit cemeteries, churches, etc. can be extremely rewarding and emotional.

> A part of my family comes from Sweden. I contacted them to arrange a visit, and after they realized that I wasn't coming to steal the family

farm, all were friendly and the details were worked out. When the door to the home was opened, a man who looked like my twin brother appeared. His grandfather and my grandfather had been brothers! Having a meal in the room where your grandfather was born was very special. Thank God my grandfather came to America. Otherwise, I might be a Swedish farmer today!

For my seventieth birthday, my daughters offered to take me anywhere in the world that I wanted to go. Much to their chagrin, I chose Pittsburgh—the city where I grew up! I wanted to revisit my old stomping ground one last time. We had a great time tracing my paper route, seeing my schools, homes, etc. We even delved into my mother's roots, amazed that her high school still had her transcripts and yearbook from 1922! We rounded out the trip with visits to some area sites—Frank Lloyd Wright's Fallingwater and the Andy Warhol Museum—and we all took in a Pirates game. A great vacation that was meaningful to me and my family.

Mike's maternal grandmother's birth house, Nyby, Sweden

Mike's maternal grandfather's birth house,
Nyssaryd, Sweden, with a distant cousin

TIME-SHARES

Many of our friends, including ourselves, owned a second, seasonal house in bygone years. Now I'm hard-pressed to know why! At some point, we reach the realization that more than one home is kind of silly, not to mention expensive! The worry and upkeep of multiple dwellings become burdensome. When one catches the travel bug, the idea of going back year after year to the same vacation house becomes boring. Transferring to an owned seasonal home is more complicated and extensive than packing for a trip. Computers, files, records—all need to be moved to the "other office." This annual ritual, though intellectually wanting, is emotionally hard to shed. We should have considered time-shares years ago!

A time-share, or fractional ownership, is often a satisfactory substitute for a second home. It meets most of the "criteria" that we have established for successful senior travel: we unpack just one time, we are not moving from place to place, and our travel to and from is predictable and familiar. You can use your shares at different locales.

With a time-share, you need not go to the same locale each time; they are available throughout the world through very reputable specialists who will want to build a long-term relationship with you just like your travel agent. The beauty of a time-share is the fact that you pay a fraction of what it would cost if you owned the place outright. Unlike a second home, it is neither a year-round worry nor expense.

HOUSE EXCHANGE

A similar concept, though not nearly as popular or as common, is a house exchange. Here, through special brokers, you permit a family to use your home and in return you use theirs.

> We have friends who own a lovely home on Coronado Island across the bay from San Diego. In the summer of 2012, they are exchanging with a family whose home is in Cambridge, England. For our friends, the motivation is to find affordable but luxurious accommodations for the summer Olympic Games. Ten members of their family will be sharing the Cambridge house for two weeks. While not inexpensive, it is certainly less than staying in a London hotel; it is also more private and laid out to permit a wonderful meeting/gathering area for a large family. The grandparents heading up this family are in their late eighties, and celebrating their sixtieth wedding anniversary.

Not everyone will attend the games every day; sometimes they will watch on TV, but the adventure can be shared in person over meals or times of quiet reflection. A special event is not required for a house exchange to work; it does satisfy the need for destination travel in some people. What is necessary for this to work well is the fact that you have *a house worth sharing in a desirable location*. In this example, the English family is tired of dreary England and wanting warm, sun-and-sand time on the Pacific Ocean. It is a win-win for everyone!

PREPARATION TO CRUISE ON AN OCEAN LINER

C ruising costs a lot of money and there are many facets involved. Preparation is the key and, as a result, unpleasant surprises can be avoided.

DECISIONS

Our first step is getting to the ship. Many wonderful cruises have a port of embarkation that is outside the United States. Always arrive in the city of embarkation the day before the ship is to sail. Often, international flights from the States arrive in Europe in the morning. Nothing is worse than arriving at your hotel around 9:00 a.m. local time and having them tell you that check-in time is 3:00 p.m.

Pay for the room in advance for the previous night, so when you arrive the room will be yours immediately. After a good four-hour sleep, when you return to the lobby for a relaxing lunch, others from your flight will be still sitting there, waiting for their room to be available for check-in! You never know what unforeseen circumstance might occur (another reason to arrive a day before sailing).

Many seniors have decided that a long flight to the embarking city is too tiring and they will only leave from a US port. Most cruises originating in the US leave from Ft. Lauderdale, Miami, Long Beach, or San Francisco. Even so, arriving a day early reduces stress and anxiety and puts you in a relaxed mood when you board. An inexpensive hotel near the pier is sufficient as a point of transition from airplane to the ship.

Whether flying overseas or domestically, we generally *do not* let the cruise line book our air travel. They most likely will book you on a circuitous routing—serving their purpose, not yours! Cruise lines will discount your cruise by hundreds of dollars to allow you to book your own air. Your travel agent will book your flights and connections that minimize total elapsed time from home.

If it is likely or highly possible that you might need to cancel, then consider letting the cruise line book your airfare. Your insurance will cost more, but if you do cancel, you will only need to deal with the cruise line and not the airline. Also, you need not pay for the entire airfare in advance. In this scenario, as previously mentioned, the cruise line will determine your routing and your seat selection on the aircraft. There are cases now where you pay a premium to the cruise line; they book your flight, but you choose the itinerary. (This is called a deviation.) Also, the cruise line sometimes offers an upgrade to business class at a very reasonable price. If booking directly with the airline, it is hard to receive a refund of cash on a nonrefundable ticket; however, the airline will give you credit for future travel within the next year.

We are all old enough now to deserve to fly business class. Whether you pay the business-class fare, upgrade from coach using frequent-flyer miles, or use miles or membership-rewards points for the total purchase, just bite the bullet and do it! You will arrive at your port of departure well fed and having had a good sleep and a relaxing flight. If we can't fly business class, we stay home until we can! It is that important.

The only exception might be is if you are flying from the States to South Africa or Australia. On these flights, a business-class ticket can cost more than $10,000, thanks to the monopolies of South African Air and Qantas. If you are traveling with your spouse, four adjoining coach seats in the middle of the cabin are quite comfortable and a fraction of the cost! (One person sits on the aisle, and the other stretches out and sleeps. After a couple of hours, you trade places.) Just be sure you receive four boarding passes, and always turn in all four on every leg of the trip. (An airline may cancel the seat reservation for the rest of the itinerary if it does not receive a boarding pass each time.)

You've heard it said, "Book at the last minute for great savings." This is hogwash! Early bookings are the best way to go before all the good stuff is taken. Also, we older folks enjoy the anticipation of planning the trip at our leisure—remember, the early bird truly gets the worm! (The only exception might be if you live in Ft. Lauderdale, Miami, or Los Angeles—keep a bag packed at all times; you can be at the pier in an hour or two and receive a 50 percent discount off the discounted price).

The first decision regarding cruising is the *size of the ship*. Choices range from small, (approximately 250 passengers) to megaliners that can accommodate thousands. As seniors, we prefer ships on the smaller side (750 to 1,250 passengers), large enough to have most all amenities, yet small enough to enter midsized ports and easier to get around when on board.

Once we have picked the ship, settled on the itinerary, and agreed to the price, the next important issue is to pick the *cabin*. Does the cabin location make much difference to us seniors? You bet it does! We want to be located midship, where all movements of the vessel are minimized and where we are near the elevators and no shipboard venue is an exhausting walk. What about the port (left) side or the starboard (right) side? Pick the side which will be closest to land most of the time—good views for morning sail-ins and the evening sail-away.

The next decision deals with the *deck number*. Pick a deck that includes concierge service, and make sure that your cabin has a veranda, or at the least, no obstructed view. Never accept a cabin at the rear of the ship where you will smell engine exhaust during the entire voyage, ship movements will be exaggerated, and everything is a very long walk. You won't need a penthouse or owner suite; the ideal cabin will be about midpoint on the pricing scale and will be much more than comfortable.

The services of the concierge are much appreciated by seniors primarily because they handle specialty restaurant reservations as well as shore-excursion bookings, private-car tours, spa reservations, etc. As a result, you can avoid long lines and fellow cruisers ahead of you in line who cannot decide what they want. Be wary of pre- and post-cruise packages sold by the cruise line. They sound great but are extremely expensive; the prices are always quoted *per person.*

PAYMENT

Normally, 10 percent of the cruise fare is due at the time of booking; airfare with seat selection is paid in full when reserving the flights, and insurance can be partially paid, or if you want to be able to cancel for *any* reason, including *preexisting conditions*, the full insurance is due at the time of booking. The balance of the cruise fare is due ninety days prior to sailing. Airlines will normally book 331 days before the flight, so it is always tricky determining exactly when to book.

SINGLE SUPPLEMENT

Single passengers are penalized when cruising. (We don't recommend traveling alone for safety reasons.)

Single fares can be double or, more often, one and a half times the per-person charge based on double occupancy. The reasons for this are that the cabins are set up for two people, and pricing has been established accordingly. One person in a cabin rather than two means less revenue for the cruise lines in the casinos, shops, bars, spas, and the destination services department. It seems unfair to penalize single travelers, but that's the way it is!

PERSONAL SAFETY ON LAND AND AT SEA

Even if we are returning to familiar territory, a long trip naturally makes one a bit apprehensive. If going overseas, has the State Department or Department of Homeland Security made any statements of caution pertaining to your intended destination? Have your newspapers or the Internet done any negative reporting lately?

More often than not, you are warned to be vigilant regarding your personal effects and jewelry when on the streets of any large, foreign city. You would, however, act no differently than you would on the streets of New York. The best place for your fine jewels is in the bank safe deposit box at home. Cash should be kept to a minimum; credit cards and bills in small denominations (American or foreign), will get you whatever you need or want.

Also carry with you a business card or matchbook cover of the hotel or ship, the address and phone number in the local language, in case you become lost. Not to the point of paranoia, but be aware of your surroundings when walking or visiting crowded tourist attractions. (I have seen gold necklaces ripped from a woman's neck before she ever left the grounds of a luxury hotel in Rio.) Pickpocketing is also prevalent in every major city of the world. Keep your wallet and camera protected in a pocket on the front of your body. It never hurts to have the address and phone number of the American embassy or consulate in your pocket (not wallet), just in case.

If aboard ship, pay close attention at the lifeboat drill, know the route from your cabin to your muster station, and don't stare into space when the equipment is being demonstrated. Testing of the emergency system should occur *before* you weigh anchor.

Shipboard crime is extremely rare, but it has received some publicity lately due to several missing person cases and the fact that no one has—or wants to have—jurisdiction to prosecute felony crimes that may have occurred at sea. Cruise lines don't want the publicity and "international waters" is cited as the reason that no one is interested in justice on the high seas.

Even when sailing in pirate-infested waters off Somalia, the cruise ships can usually outrun the pirates, and they do have procedures for dealing with these incidents if need be.

Daughter, Ardith in Cordon Bleu cooking class

"Home Away From Home"

ALL THE "NOT SO LITTLE" EXTRA CHARGES

N ow we come to all the little things that drive you crazy and increase the price.

PASSPORT AND TICKETS

First, are the passports in order and are any visas required? A passport renewal is now good for ten years but takes several weeks to process. The application for renewal and your photo can be handled by your travel agent. For an additional fee, these items can be expedited. A first-time passport will take longer, but you will be guided by your travel agent. In any event, make certain that your passport will be valid for at least six months after the return date on your ticket. Fees vary but can be over $150 per person.

Then there are the port charges/taxes and perhaps a fuel surcharge. These two items can add close to $1,000 per person to the total tab, depending upon the itinerary and length of the cruise, and are really not negotiable. You'll have more luck working toward lowering the price of the basic cruise or arranging for a *shipboard credit* of some sort for being a previous cruise guest, etc.

These are matters that a good travel agent anticipates and handles.

TRAVEL INSURANCE

Insurance is always an emotional decision. *You'll never need it until you need it!* Travel insurance is calculated considering two variables: (1) the total cost of the cruise and (2) your age. It is sold on a per-person basis.

Insurance is a wonderful profit opportunity for the insurance company and the cruise line—but not for you. *Do not insure the airfare*—the airlines will credit those tickets if you must cancel (another reason not to book air with the cruise line). Do buy the proper amount of insurance, however. There is no worse feeling than being unable to travel for whatever reason and being out of pocket $20,000 plus.

Read and understand the cancellation policy of the cruise line (terms and conditions). As a general rule, a policy that allows you to cancel for any reason should cost no more than 10 percent of the cost of the cruise without airfare; however, you may have to pay for the insurance in full at the time of booking.

Aside from protecting yourself if you have to cancel or lose property or luggage, the primary reason for buying insurance is to protect against medical problems that can occur during the trip. If needed, medevac flights for you and your companion are covered. This type of policy covers expenses which Medicare does not cover outside the United States. The charges mentioned in this chapter are part of the cost of cruising. Know what you're paying for, then just accept them and enjoy yourself—your financial concerns are now behind you.

TRANSFERS

Transfers are another add-on, the cost and method of getting to the ship from the hotel and from the ship back to the hotel or airport when it's time to disembark. The cruise line is all too happy to sell you transfers, which are priced *per person*, a big profit center for them. You will find that the local taxi company, found in front of the hotel, airport, or cruise dock, can accomplish these transfers for you and your party at a fraction of the cost charged by the cruise line. Generally, transfer by local taxi should cost about thirty-five US dollars. Also, calling your own bellman when you are ready to check out is less stressful than putting your luggage in the corridor the night before.

PRE- AND POST-CRUISE PACKAGES

You already want to arrive early for your cruise, so why not book a pre-cruise package through the cruise line?

The hotel included in such a package will cost *twice as much* as if you called the hotel directly and booked a room yourself or through your travel agent. Transfers to/from the ship will also be ridiculously high. As mentioned later, we do not recommend post-cruise packages; you will be anxious to get home by then.

> We did have a fabulous pre-river-cruise package at a chateau in Burgundy, France, where we stayed and attended a four-day cooking school, dined at Leslie Caron's restaurant, and went shopping with the chef at the town market.

A CRUISE FOR THE WHOLE FAMILY

We are talking here about a once-in-a-lifetime experience. Well planned, such cruises can be bonding experiences beyond belief. Adult seniors, their adult children, and grandchildren old enough to be responsible make up the most-likely family party. The specific cruise line selected would depend upon the age(s) of the grandchildren, family finances, and the seniors tolerance for revelry, as well as who will be paying. The choices could range from Disney, Princess, Royal Caribbean, all the way up to Crystal. The ship and itinerary should be fun for everyone.

We took a family cruise from Athens to Istanbul to celebrate the millennium. On the morning of January 1, 2000, we stood in the amphitheater in Ephesus, Turkey, where St. Paul had preached almost two thousand years before. It was a "life moment" for everyone. Speaking of life moments, these family cruises usually center around celebrating some big events—birthday, wedding anniversary, etc.

> We had a great laugh on a family cruise when transferring from the port to downtown Athens, Greece. I had reserved a private transfer for the five of us, and our transfer vehicle turned out to be similar to a Greyhound bus! My older daughter's fiancé thought that was pretty cool. Also, when we arrived at the InterContinental Hotel in Athens and only five of us got off, those standing around the portico thought that we must be celebrities!

Another recommended family cruise is to Alaska through the Inland Passage. The trip takes seven days and is most interesting in terms of wildlife sightings, scenery, and quaint little towns. Grandchildren of all ages will enjoy it, and there is enough to do in each port that no one feels as if others are clinging to them. Our family members do their own thing during the day, gather for cocktails as a group to exchange the experiences of the day, dine in the venue of their choice (often together), and gather for a game of team trivia or the show. It is up to each person to decide.

When traveling as a family, each family member updates his/her "list" of countries and islands visited. Often, at least part of an itinerary is chosen to give family members a chance to add to their list! You may obtain an up-to-date list of the countries of the world on the website *www.nationsonline.org/oneworld/countries of the world.htm*.

City Central Market, Dubrovnik, Croatia

King Alfonso XIII Hotel's Atrium
Dining Room, Seville, Spain

"Alongside," Nice, France

Taormina, Sicily, Italy

Balcony flowers, Cartagena, Columbia

Catherine the Great's Summer Palace, Pushkin, Russia

Bronze of Hans Christian Anderson, Bratislava, Slovakia

Bellvedere Palace, Vienna, Austria

Temple of Knossos, Crete, Greece

TRAVEL TIPS—THE DEVIL IS IN THE DETAILS

The only downside to cruising that I can think of is the fact that you normally get only one day per port—enough to provide an overview but certainly not an in-depth look.

Always check the number of days at sea. As we have grown older, we have come to appreciate sea days. A day at sea can pass very quickly. Between meals, you can fit in a spa treatment, workout at the gym, attend enrichment lectures, visit the ship's library, and spend internet time, among other things.

Some cruises are themed. Culinary programs and art classes are areas of concentration on certain itineraries and can be loads of fun if that is your thing. We love cooking and take classes aboard whenever they are offered. The two new Oceania ships have large demonstration kitchens with twelve individual cook stations and excellent instruction.

When a particular ship is in transition, say between the Mediterranean and the Caribbean at the end of the summer season, an itinerary will be offered for crossing the Atlantic which will include many sea days. These voyages are deeply discounted and are wonderful values if you don't mind looking at the horizon rather than a port of call! Speaking of transition, there are those who can't or don't care to fly. You can get to your port of embarkation by cruising there perhaps. Prices from New York to Southampton are reasonable. The trip is comfortable and no jetlag will be involved. All you need is time—the thing that most seniors have to spare!

All lines have evening entertainment. While this can be a pleasant way to spend part of an evening, remember, this is not Las Vegas. High quality, professional entertainment is not what cruise lines are noted for. Neither are they noted for the variety of play and excitement of their casinos. For true gamblers and entertainment lovers, Las Vegas is far superior to a cruise. The vocalist at the evening show will be leading the shuffleboard competition in the morning!

If you are cruising on a segment or two of a world cruise, be aware of "rounders." These are travelers who are cruising around the world—some practically live aboard the ship, spending up to half the year aboard. Rounders tend to stick together; they look down their collective noses at single-segment travelers. They spend most of their time playing bridge and eating in segregated fashion. Just be aware of them, and don't let them get under your skin.

The cruise director will offer a series of guest competitions each day where points can be accumulated and redeemed for prizes at the end of the trip. An example of this type activity would be Team Trivia. If you play these games, you do so for the fun and not the meager prizes. Shuffleboard and putting are other favorites.

> When on a family cruise, we five always clean up at Team Trivia. The generational difference, as well as our varied interests, seems to cover most of the categories. These games can become very competitive at times as we vie for silly vinyl bookmarks or perhaps a tote bag if we really win big!

CHRONIC HEALTH CONDITIONS

Chronic health conditions are of concern to travelers, and cruise lines are prepared to handle most anything. Most cruise ships have nurses, a doctor, and a dispensary on board, as well as set protocols and medical-evacuation plans if necessary. I have never felt safer than when aboard ship as far as my health is concerned.

Even those in need of dialysis treatments several times a week, whether for diabetes or some other kidney related disease, can be accommodated aboard ship. Just contact Dialysisatsea.com for complete information.

> We often comment that living at a continuing care retirement community is like being aboard a cruise ship, except that you never leave the pier. Well, now we have one more comparison, a few months ago we had a norovirus illness go through our community and we needed to go into "lockdown" for a few days. Sometimes you read about a cruise ship returning to port early as a result of the same thing!

Seasickness is always possible, but the advent of large stabilizers on the more-modern ships that reduce rocking and rolling to a minimum have practically eliminated it. Pills, patches, wrist bands, etc. have also been developed to combat this problem. Common sense comes into play as well. If you select an Atlantic crossing, prior to the end of hurricane season, you probably will encounter some rough seas. The Drake Passage between South America and Antarctica is an area famed for rough seas as well.

People do die on cruise ships, but again the cruise lines are prepared to help the surviving spouse. Each ship has a small morgue aboard to be used until arrangements are made.

> We have good friends who were rounders. They had no children or much extended family. The husband had a massive heart attack while the ship was in India. He was cremated there; his ashes returned to the ship and his wife kept

on cruising. This is not the typical decision in such a situation! She said, "What was the point of my going home, all of our close friends were onboard." It has been several years since he passed away, and she has taken a world-cruise each year!

In the extreme, there are those who never leave the ship. They say that all aspects of life aboard are better than what they would have ashore, and it is cheaper than a nursing home on a cost-per-day basis.

TRANSPORTATION SECURITY ADMINISTRATION

Anyone traveling in recent years is familiar with the infamous TSA, in place at all airports to keep the skies free of terrorists. The TSA is an agency of the Department of Homeland Security. Occasionally, we read about invasive body searches, aggressive pat-downs, and revealing scanning devices.

TSA policies are continuously evolving. We now have a new program called TSA Pre-Check, where for a certain fee and by providing personal information, you can by-pass regular screening and proceed through an expedited line for your security clearance. Not all airports or airlines are currently equipped to implement such a program and, anyway, the program is designed for domestic travel only at this point.

Yet another new TSA program designed for seniors over 75 will permit light jackets, belts, and shoes to be worn, rather than removed, as well as lap-tops and compliant liquids to pass through the screener without being removed from carry-on luggage.

Generally, I recommend being ready to comply with all the rules that we have reluctantly honored in recent years. First, if you are flying in the recommended Business Class, you will be eligible to use the First Class line when proceeding through security. This is a huge time-saver for starters. Beyond that, just use good common sense. You know that guns, sporting equipment, and sharp objects must be placed in checked luggage and not permitted as carry-on. Compliant liquids 3 oz. or less must be contained within a clear plastic, sealed bag and sent through the scanner separately.

I try to wear "loafer" type shoes and I carry a small plastic shoehorn in my pocket. Remember to wear pants that won't fall down when you remove your belt! If you must carry a lightweight jacket, slide it through the scanner as well.

If you are using a cane or wheelchair, the TSA personnel generally provide personal assistance. As a general guideline, *keep your eyes open and your mouth shut,* as you pass through the security checkpoint. While a bit time consuming and inconvenient, try to remember its overall purpose and try to suffer indignity as silently as possible.

TIPPING ASHORE

"Tipping" overseas can be a problem. In most cases 10 to 15 *percent* will be adequate and appreciated. Five dollars per suitcase is ample and ten dollars for the hotel concierge will be fine if he/she helps with dinner reservations, theater tickets, etc. A dollar or two for the hotel doorman as he helps unload your bags or assists in getting you a taxi will be ample. The key is to have *local currency,* which you can obtain from your local U.S. bank with about a week's notice. Also, I'd recommend having a couple hundred dollars in U.S. currency as emergency back-up. So far, the world seems to still like *green backs.* When on local tours, a gratuity is often included in the price of your ticket; however, an additional couple of *bucks,* for the memorable guide will be much appreciated.

We have already covered the use of credit cards as our primary means of making foreign purchases, especially since you have notified your credit card company/ies of your dates of travel and itinerary. An ATM debit card can also come in handy, but good planning should preclude the need to use one.

GENERAL COMPORTMENT

Less than in years past, but still we are sometimes thought of as *Ugly Americans* when we are traveling abroad. Americans don't set out to offend; it's just that our customs are different. We need to try to be *extra* polite. It is good to learn and remember a few key phrases in a foreign language: good morning, thank you, have a nice day, etc. These attempts will be much appreciated. We tend to over complain when our hotel accommodations are not perfect—if you have twin beds, and ordered a *king*, just push the beds together! There is no need to alert management.

TAXI

Taxi! Don't attempt to hail a cab mid-block or *on the run*. It is best to engage a taxi at a taxi stand or at a hotel. The doorman can explain your destination to the driver and verify the anticipated fare. Many taxis in major world capitals now are equipped to take credit cards. Try to find taxis with a *working meter!* As previously mentioned, carry a business card naming your hotel, its address and phone number whenever you are in unfamiliar territory and/or don't speak the local language.

PROPER APPAREL ASHORE

Finally, don't dress in a manner that will call attention to yourself: halter dresses, shorts, sneakers, tee-shirts with slogans, flags, etc. are dead giveaways that Americans are coming and that they are disrespectful of the local morays. Visiting museums, cathedrals, churches, and historic sites overseas, require conservative dress, even though such might not be the case at home. The general rule—try to blend in and call as little attention to yourself as possible.

PHOTOGRAPHY

No longer is it necessary to have all kinds of equipment strung around your neck: light meters, zoom lenses, back-up cameras, etc. We now live in the digital age and, thankfully, cameras are a part of this new technology! We have the capacity to see whether or not the picture that we just took is the shot we want. If not, take another one. Be patient, you will get your unobstructed shot! Camera cases, tripods and the like are no longer part of the scene at popular photo sites around the world. A digital camera is a must, if for no other reason than rolls of film need not be purchased and made a part of your luggage.

SIGHT-SEEING VIA BUS

The tour bus is a very popular mode of transportation for seniors attempting to gain an overview of the surrounding area or an in-depth city tour. Often the bus will unload tourists at point A and pick them up at a designated time at point B. A good tour will emphasize the importance of being at the pick-up point promptly on time. Passengers who are late will need to return to their ship or hotel on their own.

> *We were enjoying a lovely walking tour through the center of Aix-en-Provence and had been told by our driver to be at the garden fountain at the other end of the esplanade at 2:30, approximately ½ mile from the drop off point. Two couples were not accounted for at the time of departure and the bus left without them! The taxi from Aix to the ship in Marseilles cost more than $150 per couple! They never missed a bus again.*

If your bus makes quick stops for photos, don't be the party that is always in the gift shop buying mementos and forcing the others on your bus to wait for you. This is the ultimate in rude and inconsiderate behavior and it will not endear you to your fellow passengers.

Usually there are no *reserved seats*, except for a few seats for the handicapped near the front of the bus. Do not use these seats unless you are truly handicapped and find moving through the bus extremely difficult. It is customary to take the *same seat* that you had before exiting the bus for your photo or rest stop, even though the seat is not reserved. If you have favorite seats, then get down to the bus departure point early to be one of the first to board the bus initially.

ANCHORS AWEIGH, FINALLY ON THE SHIP!

L ook! There is the ship! We are finally boarding. It seems as if we have been planning this for months and the time has now arrived. Bon Voyage and Welcome Aboard!

SHORE EXCURSIONS

Shore excursions are one of the primary reasons for cruising. Although not much time is spent in each port, shore excursions do provide an overview of cities, surrounding areas, and cultures. Seniors must be quite discerning when selecting excursions to determine the total time of the excursions (a half day is plenty) and to assess the degree of difficulty in the context of their own capabilities. Usually, excursions are rated *moderate, vigorous, or easy*, or words to that effect. Extended walking, climbing, rough terrain (loose rocks or cobblestones), etc. are usually mentioned, with warnings that passengers with specifically listed limitations or conditions should avoid certain excursions. In each port of call, there are a number of excursion choices, often eight or ten. There will be choices within each category of difficulty, and the total elapsed time will be mentioned.

Shore excursions are relatively expensive; however, some cruises say that they are "free," meaning that they are included in the base cruise price. Generally, excursions can be booked online prior to sailing. I would recommend that you book one or two from home those that you most want or think will be the most popular. Play it by ear from there; once on board, book depending upon how you are feeling. Most often, bookings can be made a day in advance, although some offerings could be sold out. The most expensive excursions usually involve extreme activities: dog sledding on glaciers, scuba diving, kayaking, zip-lining, parasailing—things better left to the younger generation. There will be a large contingent on board who will take delight in reminding all who will listen that they walked ashore, hired a driver, and saved a ton of money! Perhaps they did, but what did they truly learn?

> We were in line waiting to enter the Alhambra in Granada, Spain, when a group from our ship, after a two-hour train ride, booked independently, found out that the Alhambra was sold out for the day! We, of course, proceeded with the tour that the ship had arranged!

The cruise line has checked out all of the tour operators that they use and have contracted for very comfortable coaches and knowledgeable English-speaking guides. Individual admissions to museums and attractions along the way have been included in your tour price. If you are on a ship's tour, you will not have the ship sail away without you! If that happens, your privately hired driver will become extremely expensive! It will require a costly last-minute flight to catch the ship in the next port of call.

Cruise lines often bundle four or five tours and offer them at some discounted price. I would avoid succumbing to this temptation. Toward the end of the cruise, you may be tired and prefer to spend the day on board. Some general impressions: cruise lines usually "rate" their excursions as a bit easier than I have found them to be and also a bit longer than advertised. A three-hour morning tour utilizing a motor coach and some relatively easy walking will make the venue or sights more interesting because you'll be able to enjoy the trip. You will also be back aboard for a wonderful lunch and a refreshing nap before tea time.

Most often, there will be plenty of room on the coach (also equipped with a lavatory). All seats are seldom filled. If you want to see sights by yourself, I would recommend that you have the ship arrange for a private car and driver, rather than trying to do this yourself on the pier.

> We have negotiated a fixed price for a tour of a certain length to see city sights and surroundings. The driver's ability to speak English and his knowledge of the sites are critical to your enjoying and relaxing during this experience. You can judge this ability when you are negotiating with the driver. The ship, through its recommendation, has pre-screened the driver for reliability. Often, these privately escorted sightseeing adventures turn out to be highlights of the journey.

CUISINE ABOARD THE SHIP

Cruising and fine dining are thought of as synonymous— so much food, so little time, with food 24/7. In addition to the main restaurant, most ships have specialty dining venues—Italian, Asia-Pacific, French, steak/chops to name a few. Atmosphere in these restaurants is more intimate, quieter, and more relaxing. You will want to try them all if for no other reason than to break the monotony of the same dining room for seven or more nights. Usually, there is no additional charge for these specialty venues and, again, the concierge near your stateroom will handle your reservation requests.

Dining at sea is an informal experience these days on most cruise lines—no tuxedos, no set tables. You dine when you want, with whom you want, and a jacket at the evening meal is optional. Choosing to sit at a table of eight is a wonderful way to meet people, or you can say that it is "date night" and have a table for two. Breakfast, lunch, and dinner are generally served in the main dining room, plus a much less-formal, but bountiful, buffet is available throughout the day and evening, often located on an outside terrace. Food is always available near the pool, and room service usually is available 24/7. Teatime is very popular and is available every afternoon, featuring finger sandwiches, scones, and other tasty desserts. All of this food is included in the cruise fare, so older travelers must discipline themselves; otherwise, it would be very easy to gain ten pounds!

> We travel with Oceania or Regent, both rated highly by frequent travelers. We like them because the ships are relatively small, very informal, and the cuisine is excellent. We have not been on Crystal, although it has been rated no.1 by travelers for the past seventeen years. Crystal is more formal and expensive than our choices. Overall, on a value for money basis, neither Oceania nor Regent can be beaten.

ALCOHOLIC BEVERAGES

Alcoholic beverages are handled differently, depending upon the cruise company. Some lines have all-inclusive pricing, so alcohol has been included in the cruise price. Other lines price alcohol on an ala carte basis. Best to find out the policy prior to booking, then select the line whose policy best suits your lifestyle. We are not big drinkers, so prefer ala carte pricing on drinks. I can't personally drink enough to make it pay for me, and I don't enjoy subsidizing other people's drinking.

GRATUITIES

Gratuities are another personal item, in my opinion. I do not like cruise lines that include gratuities in one overall price. Other lines apply a "recommended gratuity" to your final statement. I philosophically oppose others telling me what to tip. Generally, I reduce the recommended amount and give additional tips personally to those who have rendered me excellent service. I don't embrace the concept of gratuity sharing with all those ship employees who the passengers never see. If the guys in the boiler room depend on tips to augment their wages to a subsistence level, they should either be paid a higher wage or find a better-paying job!

SHOPPING

A big reason people cruise and travel is that they love to shop. Some use this opportunity to buy fine jewelry from around the world. Usually the ship's cruise director can recommend reputable stores and shops in each port of call. Passengers sometimes receive discounts by shopping in stores that the cruise line recommends. Each country and port is famous for something—leather, jewels, baskets, art glass, etc. Try to buy items that are unique to that locale and not something that can be found all along the itinerary. Remember, you will probably never be back that way again. Do you really like and want the item? Will it ever require service or repair? Is it too large to carry aboard? If you truly love it, by all means, buy it!

In many world ports, *haggling* is just a normal part of the shopping scene.

> For example, in Istanbul, no one ever pays the first price mentioned. I cannot stand haggling, but my wife loves it; therefore, she does most of the shopping overseas!

Here is a shopping tip when traveling far away: *alert* your credit card companies of your itinerary prior to leaving home. This way, when they see a large amount being charged overseas, they will know that it is you. Theft of cards has made the companies far more cautious for your protection, as well as their own. If they know where you will be traveling and when, the embarrassment and frustration of being delayed while they verify who is making the charge can be avoided.

One *cardinal rule* when traveling; *never* promise to shop for people back home when traveling overseas. You will waste precious time and still not know whether the purchase you make on their behalf is what they really want. Shipping and possible return problems are vacation spoilers—stay clear of them.

COLLECTING

Often, cruising gives you the opportunity to enhance your collection of almost anything imaginable. For example, my wife and I collect studio-blown art glass. We have been adding to this collection for more than thirty years and find cruising a wonderful way to find unique and beautiful pieces.

Italy, Sweden, Ireland, France, Portugal, the Czech Republic, and Germany are among many countries that have long histories of producing great decorative glass. Often, on these trips we have had the opportunity to meet the artist who created the work that we wanted to acquire. We always have new pieces shipped to our home in the States, and we pay only by credit card, thus protecting ourselves against any loss, breakage, or substitution (there is no duty to be paid on original art). With glass, like fine painting or sculpting, the artist's signature engraved into the piece protects the authenticity and thus the value. We have received much pleasure over the years by looking at pieces, remembering where they were purchased and the artist who created this one-of-a-kind art object. Professional packing, shipping, and worldwide acceptance of credit cards have made the collecting of practically anything and everything possible. The anticipation of a new addition to your collection adds additional excitement to the cruise experience itself. Oceania's new ship, the *Marina*, uses art glass as its major decorative theme. Crystal banisters made by the French company Lalique are absolutely stunning.

> We visited the Orrefors factory in Sweden during the one hundredth anniversary of the company. Master blowers were allowed to create unique pieces for the celebration. We were fortunate enough to buy a lovely multicolored blue vase signed by the artist and engraved no. 1 of one.

SOUVENIRS

Who is not into the purchase of mementos representing one's travels? As soon as you disembark into the next port, the vendors meet you on the pier, selling everything imaginable. You buy to create a memory or for something to take to the grandchildren. Try to keep in mind: is there room in your luggage for these T-shirts and caps? Do I really want to clutter up my customs declaration with this junk? Will I or the family ever look at this stuff again once I bring it home?

Shipboard boutiques are a good source for quality souvenirs, although there are seldom bargains to be found on board.

> Once, while in Hong Kong, we purchased the Little Red Book, the *Thoughts of Chairman Mao*, while visiting the border between the New Territories and Communist mainland China. The book was later confiscated at Australian immigration along with my copy of *Playboy*! So be careful when on the hunt for souvenirs.

FOREIGN FOOD ON SHORE

Since this book is about international travel sites and travel tips, I would be remiss not to say a word or two about foreign food. Experiencing new foods is an important part of the travel adventure/experience. Like everything else, *moderation* is the key. Try to be careful of unfamiliar spices and rich sauces. Attempt to learn a few menu items in the native language.

> On our first trip to France, for the first few days, we only knew *jambon* and *fromage*! We ate our fill of ham and cheese sandwiches. Wiener schnitzel in Germany is not a hot dog!

Upon request, menus are often available in English. A good dining tip: carry Tums with you at all times! Of course, if you are on a cruise, ocean or river, this should not be a problem. I have found it to be more satisfying to try a native dish rather than ordering a foreign attempt at something American—a hamburger, for example!

GREAT SITES FOR SENIORS

This list of places and sites is by no means all inclusive. These are places that I remember were well suited to a senior, regardless of his/her limitations. Most of these I visited after having had a stroke, quintuple bypass heart surgery, rheumatoid arthritis, diabetes (insulin dependency), cataract, hand, and gall bladder surgery. They were all fun to see, provided lasting memories, and are sights that I would enjoy seeing again. By design, I have not included sights in the United States.

NORTH AMERICA

❑ Quebec City, Quebec: the fabulous Chateau Frontenac Hotel, the St. Lawrence River as viewed from the Plains of Abraham—as French as it gets in North America

❑ Vancouver, British Columbia: Chinatown, Stanley Park, and the Pan Pacific Cruise Ship Terminal.

In the dining room of the Pan Pacific Hotel, prior to boarding our ship, I spotted another couple having lunch. I asked if they too would be boarding.

"No," they said, "we just got off."

My wife asked, "What was your favorite shore excursion?"

They said, "Taking the helicopter to the top of the glacier-mountain in Juneau and dog-sledding on the glacier!"

That little query cost me $369. I, in turn, went whale watching!

❑ Victoria, British Columbia: high tea at the Empress Hotel, the boat tour of the harbor, Butchart Gardens, the provincial government buildings

SOUTH AMERICA

❑ Buenos Aires, Argentina: a wonderful and diverse city coach tour, luxurious residential areas, Evita Peron's tomb, dinner and a tango-dancing show

❑ Cartagena, Columbia: an old-town and fortressed area well preserved from colonial times, beautiful beaches and modern skyscrapers, perfect for a city tour

❏ Montevideo, Uruguay: a gorgeous, marble Palacio Legislativo (parliament building), urban-city streets (commercial and residential) reminiscent of Paris, beautiful beaches within the city center, the nearby town of Punta del Este—the "Riviera of South America (beaches, condos, racing cars, and clubs), the most modern (in architectural design) airport in the Western Hemisphere , the Carrasco International Airport.

❏ Rio de Janeiro, Brazil: the outstretched arms of Christ the Redeemer high above the city, a picnic on Sugarloaf Mountain overlooking the harbor, the beaches of Ipanema and Copacabana

"Air-boating" in Belize

Aerial Tram through rain forest, Puerto Limon, Costa Rica

Friendly sloth, Cartagena, Columbia

Hand Sculpture, Punta del Este, Uruguay

Evita Peron's tomb, Buenos Aires, Argentina

"Pink White House," Buenos Aires, Argentina

AFRICA

- ❑ Cape Town, South Africa: Table Mountain, high tea at the Mount Nelson Hotel, Robbens Island—where Nelson Mandela was imprisoned for twenty-seven years, Cape of Good Hope, the rough mixing of the Atlantic and Indian oceans, penguins

- ❑ Casablanca, Morocco: the second largest mosque in the Muslim world, ride a camel (yes, seniors can!)

- ❑ Tangier, Morocco: the Casbah and the Medina, the homes of Malcolm Forbes and Doris Duke

- ❑ Johannesburg, South Africa: Soweto, homes of Nelson Mandela and Bishop Desmond Tutu, the Apartheid Museum

- ❑ Thornybush, South Africa, or any five-star safari accommodation, where you have the chance to see the Big Five (lion, leopard, Cape buffalo, rhino, and elephant).

Table Mountain, Cape Town, South Africa

"Seniors Ride Camels Too," Casablanca, Morocco

Political Prison, (held Nelson Mandela for 27
years), Robbens Island, South Africa

Actual former political prisoner guiding
the tour at Robbens Island

Hassan II Mosque, second largest in the
world, Casablanca, Morocco

Sunset cruise on the Zambezi River, Livingstone, Zambia

Sharing the pool, Hotel Livingstone, Victoria Falls, Zambia

"Friends Met on Safari," Thornybush, South Africa

"End of the World in Africa,"
Cape of Good Hope, South Africa

ASIA

Other than Tokyo, Hong Kong, and Singapore, all of which have wonderful sights for seniors from any vantage point, and perhaps Kuala Lumpur for the Petronas Twin Towers and the ability to observe the melding of Chinese, Indian, and Malay cultures in actual harmony, I am reluctant to recommend other Asian cities because signs in English are very limited, the culture is so different, and the indigenous foods are so foreign. Many Asian cities are for the younger generation! It has been a few years since I visited Asia and undoubtedly it is more *"tourist friendly"* today than it used to be. Still, I don't consider it an *easy visit* for Seniors.

> Partially, I am prejudiced when it comes to Asia having spent so much time there on business. For reasons already stated, I have had no desire to return. There was a time (more than fifteen years), when I wouldn't even eat Chinese food.
>
> Once, when returning from Japan, my hosts had given me a departing wrapped gift which they said was a "traditional Japanese crock." When American customs opened it, we discovered that it was an ornate *clock*! While I sorted that out with customs—who saw no humor in it, for

about forty-five minutes, my wife and children wondered why I hadn't exited the customs hall!

AUSTRALIA

❑ Sydney, New South Wales: The Opera House, the Harbor Bridge, Bondi Beach, and the city coach and harbor tours are all sights to behold.

EUROPE

❑ Amsterdam, Holland: a ride through the canals, Anne Frank's house, the windmills, the Van Gogh Museum, the State Museum (Rijksmuseum with all the Rembrandts)

❑ Athens, Greece: the view of the Acropolis and Parthenon from any hotel rooftop bar in town, the Olympic Stadium, Hadrian's Gate, the agora, the Plaka district.

❑ Barcelona, Spain: everything Antoni Guadi, wonderful city tour, Picasso Museum, tapas for dinner (who can wait until 10:30 p.m. when the locals have their dinner?)

❑ Berlin, Germany: Brandenburg Gate, the Reichstag (take an elevator to the glass-domed roof and walk around the base), the Berlin Wall,

Checkpoint Charlie, a gourmet dinner on the second floor of the Hotel Adlon overlooking the Brandenburg Gate (where Michael Jackson hung his son over the balcony)

❑ Bergen, Norway: the picturesque harbor, home of composer Edvard Grieg

❑ Bilbao, Spain: Frank Gehry's Guggenheim Museum

❑ Bratislava, Slovakia: bronze statues throughout downtown, including Andy Warhol (considered a native son although born in Pittsburgh)

❑ Budapest, Hungary: the Hungarian Parliament, the busy Danube River, oversight from Buda (the Fisherman's Bastion), the funicular from Buda down to the Danube and across the bridge to Pest

❑ Cologne, Germany: the wonderful Gothic cathedral especially viewed from the river, the majestic bridge over the Rhine where a train appears every ninety seconds, a beer and brat in any ale house

❑ Copenhagen, Denmark: the incomparable Tivoli Gardens, the Little Mermaid guarding the harbor, the royal palace and the changing of the guards, the magnificent bridge-tunnel to Malmo, Sweden

❑ Dresden, Germany: all important downtown buildings and churches reconstructed after World War II, site of Kurt Vonnegut's *Slaughterhouse-Five*

❑ Dublin, Ireland: the Guinness brewery, Trinity College

❑ Edinburgh, Scotland: the Edinburgh Castle

❑ Florence, Italy: the *David* at the Accademia Gallery, Ponte Vecchio bridge, the Uffizi Gallery

❑ Geneva, Switzerland: the tranquility of Lake Geneva, any restaurant where the server is taking orders in French, German, Italian, and English—all at the same time (amazing!)

❑ Gibraltar, United Kingdom: watching all the Barbary monkeys masturbate on the Rock of Gibraltar, tour of the tunnels where Eisenhower held WWII meetings

❑ Giverny, France: the home and inspirational gardens of Claude Monet

❑ Granada, Spain: the Moorish fortress the Alhambra

- ❑ Helsinki, Finland: the Church of the Rock, Olympic stadium, all the very contemporary architecture and design.

- ❑ Istanbul, Turkey: the Blue Mosque, the Bosphorus Straits, the dinner show to see the whirling dervishes, Hagia Sophia mosque, the Grand Bazaar

- ❑ Lisbon, Portugal: Monument of the Navigators (the Discoveries), Belem Tower, Barrio Alta, Alfama, the Tagus River, Atlantis glass native to Portugal (we purchased a beautiful crystal figurine here)

- ❑ London, England: Big Ben, Houses of Parliament, Westminster Abbey, London Eye, Piccadilly Circus, Trafalgar Square, Buckingham Palace, any double-decker bus ride, high tea at the Ritz Hotel.

- ❑ Mainz, Germany: the Gutenberg Museum and Bible (Martin Luther translated this Bible from the original Latin into German, thus unifying the many German states under one language and forming the Protestant religion.)

- ❑ Milan, Italy: *The Last Supper*, La Scala Opera House, the Duomo di Milano, Galleria Vittorio Emanuel

- ❑ Monte Carlo, Monaco: the Casino de Monte Carlo (there is an admission fee), the boats in the harbor, the "beautiful people," an evening sail-away, the elevators taking you from harbor side up to the city

- ❑ Munich, Germany: the Hofbrauhaus, the BMW factory

- ❑ Normandy, France: Normandy American Cemetery and Memorial where thousands of American soldiers rest in peace from the D-Day invasion, June 6, 1944

- ❑ Oslo, Norway: the National Museum of Contemporary Art (a bit racy!), home of Henrik Ibsen, Vigeland Park, the Viking Ship Museum

- ❑ Paris, France: Notre Dame, Eiffel Tower, Montmartre, the Louvre Museum, Musee d'Orsay, any Left Bank (Rive Gauche) bistro or café

In London and Paris, you can trust the taxis. From our hotel in Paris, we were going to dinner. My mother and I in one taxi and my wife and our daughters in another; the two taxis took off in opposite directions. Voila! In ten minutes, both cabs pulled up at the restaurant at the same time!

We would definitely recommend Tour d'Argent as one of Paris' finest restaurants—most famous for Duckling. Mine was duck #639,978. They also sell crystal ducks in the gift shop. The duck dinner for two and the crystal duck cost the same—$300 (in 1996).

❑ Pisa, Italy: the Leaning Tower.

❑ Prague, Czech Republic: a city bus tour, the Prague Castle, Old Town, the Charles Bridge, the Czech White House, St. Vitus Cathedral

Always on the hunt for new pieces of glass, we had visited all the major glass stores (Moser to Bohemian antique glass) while in Prague and, on our final night, found a gallery that was open until 1:00 a.m. It was part of a Thai restaurant owned by an architect/glass blower who had redecorated the Czech White House. We weren't expecting much but found a wonderful piece that has become one of our cherished prizes.

❑ Rome, Italy: the Vatican, St. Peter's Basilica, Pantheon, Trevi Fountain, Coliseum, Sistine Chapel, the Forum, the Spanish Steps (to sit and people watch, not climb!)

- ❏ Rouen, France: the cathedral painted by Monet, the site of the burning of Joan of Arc

- ❏ Seville, Spain: the Jewish Quarter, the Seville Cathedral (third largest in the world), tomb of Christopher Columbus, paella in the King Alphonso XIII Hotel lobby atrium

- ❏ Stockholm, Sweden: sailing in among the many small islands, Old Town (Gamla stan), Vasa Museum, a building built around a seventeenth-century warship which sank in Stockholm harbor, Olympic Stadium, Stockholm City Hall (home of the Nobel Prizes, except the Peace Prize which is awarded from Oslo), Millesgarden

- ❏ St. Petersburg, Russia: the Hermitage Museum, the Kirov Ballet, Catherine the Great's summer palace (town of Pushkin), an evening with Rasputin at the Osipov Palace where he was killed

- ❏ Tallinn, Estonia: the city center McDonald's of which all of Estonia is extremely proud, the sweater market, the National "Singing" Stadium

- ❏ Venice, Italy: St. Mark's Square, Murano Island (glass blowing), Doge Palace, Bridge of Sighs, canals and gondolas, the Peggy Guggenheim Museum on the Grand Canal, the water taxis

- ❑ Vienna, Austria: order a Sachertorte at the Hotel Sacher, St. Stephen's Cathedral, a concert of chamber music featuring Mozart, Wagner, and Beethoven in a palace that was Mozart's home

- ❑ Zurich, Switzerland: exquisite shopping for watches and fine gold jewelry

Rijksmuseum, Amsterdam Holland

"Main Street," Amsterdam, Holland

Joan Miro Foundation, overlooking Barcelona, Spain

Designed by Antoni Gaudi, Barcelona, Spain

Parc Guelle, Barcelona, Spain

Brandenberg Gate, the Wall is gone! Berlin, Germany

"Check Point Charlie," entering the
American Sector, Berlin, Germany

Part of the Wall still stands, Berlin, Germany

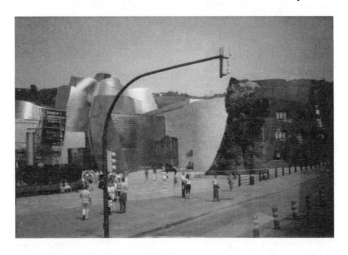

The Guggenheim Museum and the "Pup," Bilboa, Spain

The funicular from Buda to Pest, and
vice versa, Budapest, Hungary

"Two lovely Mermaids," Copenhagen, Denmark

Tivoli Gardens, Denmark's Disneyland, Copenhagen

"As Pretty as a Painting," Monet's Giverny Gardens, France

The Alhambra Fortress, Granada, Spain

Topkapi Palace, Istanbul, Turkey

Hagia Sophia, has been a church and a
mosque; now a museum, Istanbul Turkey

Whirling Dervishes, Istanbul, Turkey

Grand Bazaar, Istanbul, Turkey

Belem Tower, Lisbon, Portugal

American Cemetery, Normandy, France

Vigeland Park, Oslo, Norway

Eiffel Tower, Paris, France

Sacre Coeur, Montmarte, Paris, France

Louvre Museum, Paris France

Holding up the "Leaning Tower," Pisa, Italy

St. Nicholas Church, Old Town Square,
Prague, Czech Republic

"Monet's Rouen," Rouen Cathedral, Rouen, France

Church of the Spilled Blood, St. Petersburg, Russia

Summer Palace of Catherine the Great, Pushkin, Russia

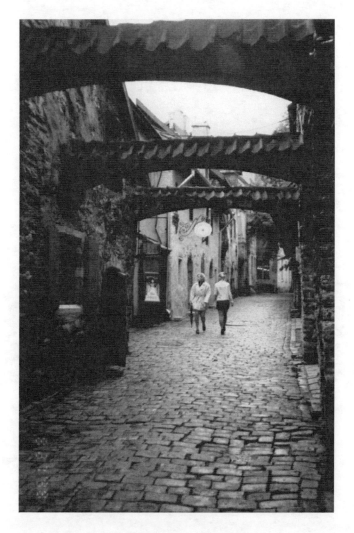

Estonians out shopping, Tallinn, Estonia

Hermitage Museum, St. Petersburg, Russia

Celsus Library, Ephesus, Turkey

St. Mark's Square, Venice, Italy

Rialto Bridge, Venice, Italy

Bridge of Sighs, Venice, Italy

St. Paul's Amphitheater, Ephesus, Turkey

"World of Rugs," Kasadasi, Turkey

As mentioned at the top, this is not an all-inclusive list by any means. Each of these cities does have excellent shopping and multiple sites that are easily accessible by seniors. It goes without saying, these cities also offer delicious and a wide variety of national cuisine!

PLACES THAT I WANTED TO GO, BUT IT IS TOO LATE NOW

China, Cairo, Jerusalem, Abu Dhabi, Dubai, Amman, Damascus, and Moscow were all considered in earlier times, but for a number of different reasons, we didn't make it there. These are not easy trips for seniors, and my window of opportunity has closed. Perhaps not for you though. In my case, they have been erased from my bucket list, and I no longer think about them!

PLACES THAT I NEVER WANTED TO GO!

While popular with many, I'm not turned on by India, Burma, Saudi Arabia, Iraq, Iran, Cambodia, Vietnam, and Laos. Friends who have gone there, often have come home sick, sometimes having contracted something quite serious. I've never considered these places worth the risk. (I'll read about them and look at pictures.)

HAWAII—A PARTICULARLY GOOD DESTINATION FOR SENIORS

The Hawaiian Islands deserve a chapter all their own in any travel book geared toward seniors even if the main thrust of this book is international travel. While Hawaii is a US state, it is "faraway" and quite exotic. For seniors, it is a perfect venue—same money, same language, great weather, familiar accommodations, "American tourists" are liked and appreciated, and it is easy to get there (especially if you live on or near the West Coast).

Whether Oahu or an outer island is your destination, the airlines serving Honolulu have done a wonderful job of making the transfer as seamless as possible. Now there are a number of flights to several islands that are nonstop from many mainland departure cities. Each of the major islands has its distinct personality. Whether you like hiking, golf, volcanoes, beaches, military history, sightseeing, shopping, or just relaxing at your resort hotel, the Hawaiian Islands has it all.

The other advantage of Hawaii is that it's a popular spot for the whole family. One of our more-inspired Christmas celebrations was a family trip to the Big Island. We rented a condo, and everyone could come and go as they pleased. The trip itself was our big present to one another. The reduced stress of not having to worry about buying and wrapping gifts was one of the best parts of the trip. A few macadamia nut stocking stuffers purchased at the local drug store was all we needed. Nothing like a luau for Christmas dinner and whale watching instead of shoveling snow!

Usually, visitors to Hawaii are there for a week. If they leave home early in the morning, there will still be some hours of daylight when they arrive. The return trip is usually an overnight flight, giving you that last day in Hawaii to enjoy yourself. Many find the familiarity of Hawaii so inviting, that total relaxation is easily achievable. Often, airlines, hotels, and rental-car companies put package deals together which are very attractive. The weather is fine year round, so go at your convenience.

We lived on Oahu for three years right after Hawaii achieved statehood. One of our daughters was born there. While Oahu has seen remarkable changes over the past fifty years, it is still alluring and the outer tourist islands have remained quite natural. We have returned to Hawaii many times and will continue to do so, as it is our favorite travel destination in the world on many different levels.

> When we first arrived in 1960, we took the bus from our apartment in Waipahu into Honolulu (now a fifteen-minute trip on the freeway). It took more than an hour weaving through all the little sugarcane towns. We asked each other, "How and why did this place become a state?" Now we know!

USS Arizona Memorial, Pearl Harbor, Oahu, Hawaii

OTHER ISLANDS OF THE WORLD

Again, not an all-inclusive list, but these islands are often visited by cruise ships; others are destination islands and thus worthy of mention.

- ❑ The Caribbean Islands and the Bahamas: near to the US mainland, great weather, used to handling large groups of tourists, easy to reach from the US mainland

- ❑ New Zealand: The two main islands are very diverse, from snow-capped peaks to fjords and beaches, agriculture, sheep herding, and native arts and crafts.

- ❑ Malta: very picturesque, has a convoluted history, Valletta—a good walking town, Caravaggio's *The Beheading of St. John the Baptist*

- ❑ Rhodes: The *Colossus* is gone, but evidence of the Knights Templar and other crusaders are still around.

- ❑ Crete: the Palace of Knossos—center of Minoan civilization, Mt. Ida, and very early evidence of Western civilization

- ❑ Majorca/Menorca: a gorgeous harborside cathedral, the monastery where Chopin and George Sand were lovers, the place where mayonnaise was invented

- ❑ Jamaica: Montego Bay, Ocho Rios, lush mountains and rainforests

- ❑ Puerto Rico: from the posh resorts to historical forts and major industry, all blended together

- ❑ Hispaniola: the dichotomy of the Dominican Republic and Haiti sharing an island

- ❑ Tahiti: Paul Gauguin is alive and well in Papeete! The Gauguin Museum has no original paintings, only copies!

- ❑ The Falkland Islands: a bit of Britain off the coast of Argentina, don't miss teatime! Several fascinating penguin colonies, a nice stop on a cruise if weather permits—one day is quite sufficient.

We think that these islands would be of particular interest to seniors. They are not too difficult to traverse, and within an hour or two, provide a genuine look at a way of life other than our own.

MASTER CHECKLISTS

BEFORE LEAVING HOME

1. Stop newspapers and mail.
2. Lock all windows and doors.
3. Turn off main water line.
4. Adjust thermostat.
5. Turn off and unplug electric items and computers.
6. Alert family as to your itinerary.
7. Alert your credit card companies of your itinerary.
8. If leaving the country, register your destinations with the State Department in case of emergency at www.travelregistration.state.gov.

READY FOR THE TRIP

1. Documents in hand: passports, visas, confirmations, travel insurance contract
2. Airline and/or ship tickets
3. Medicines/toiletries packed
4. Clothes packed

5. Cameras/phone/chargers

6. Photocopy of your passport/visas; list of credit card numbers and telephone contact; list of medications; driver's license, *put into a separate bag from the items themselves.*

7. "Extras" packed—teeth, glasses, hearing aids, etc.

8. Current picture ID for identification (driver's license), and/or passport

9. Reconfirm pickup time with driver to the airport

10. If cruising, have ship's luggage tags/cabin number on every piece of luggage.

11. Carry-on/tote bag ready, perhaps include an extra set of underwear, and a light jacket, if enough room!

12. One final check of *all documents* needed for the trip

AT THE AIRPORT

1. Tip money handy

2. Ticket/boarding pass and ID ready

3. Request a wheelchair

4. Collect luggage claim checks from the airline

5. Zip through security with Boarding Pass in Hand

6. Arrive at the Gate with an hour to spare

7. Buy snacks and reading material

8. Use the Rest Room

9. Put on compression stockings to help circulation on flight.

ONCE ABOARD THE PLANE

1. Settle in—get comfortable.

2. Exercise at your seat and by walking around every hour or two.

3. Happy flying!

DISEMBARKING THE PLANE

1. Get your wheel chair.

2. Get your luggage.

3. Find your transportation to the hotel or ship.

TAKING A CRUISE

Arriving at the Port (Ship)

1. Turn in your luggage and proceed to early check-in.

2. Turn in your passport (always keep a copy of the main passport page in your wallet).

3. Obtain the keys to your cabin.

4. Enjoy lunch while you wait for your cabin to be available.

5. Take the luggage from the passageway into your cabin

6. Unpack everything.

7. Familiarize yourself with the in-suite safe, minibar, light controls, TV, etc.

8. Try on the life vests.

9. Arrange dinner reservations via the concierge.

10. Check on prebooked shore excursions with destination services.

11. Take a walk around the ship to learn the shortest way to important venues.

12. Take a nap!

13. Time for the lifeboat drill—go to your assigned muster station,

14. Have a cocktail and enjoy the 6:00 p.m. sail-away.

15. Enjoy dinner!

16. Bon Voyage!

Hopefully, you have found these travel tips and checklists helpful and soothing enough to make you want to continue traveling well into your eighties! It is strictly a matter of desire, coupled with sufficient time to plan and sufficient money, to avoid the pitfalls of travel that make the experience so frustrating. An itinerary that is within your means, psychologically, physically, and economically, will be a trip that is enjoyed and one that will be long and fondly remembered. The retelling of your adventures to family and friends will make you the life of the party until your next trip. You needn't tromp through ancient ruins (Pompeii, etc.) to be the focal point of conversation.

It has been a fun travel experience writing this book. I hope that you have enjoyed it and learned a few new things that will make traveling easier for you and your family.

Healthy, happy, and safe travels—keep the ball rolling!

P.S. I forgot to get you home!

GOING HOME

When the main event of the trip is over, it is time to go home! Try to avoid the temptation to book a post-cruise extra day or two at your cruise destination city, or an extra stay in London after Wimbledon, for example. These kinds of extra days sound wonderful six or more months before the trip, but when the time comes, going directly home is often more appealing.

The key to arriving home less than wiped out with your vacation/trip ruined is to book travel home with the minimum amount of elapsed time. If you are departing from Europe, the first objective is to secure a nonstop flight to the United States. If you will be changing planes at your US disembarkation point, study the connecting flights carefully. Staying on the same airline that brought you across the Atlantic is helpful from a luggage transfer standpoint—a business/first-class lounge or club should be available as well.

If after arriving in the United States you need to fly to the West Coast, you may consider staying over for a night and returning home the next day. We like to leave Europe as early in the day as possible, arriving with as much daylight remaining as possible. This gives time to clear immigration and customs, transfer luggage, and make your connecting flight before it gets dark. Once aboard the final leg, relax and get some sleep. If we can make it home from Europe to Phoenix in less than twenty-four hours of elapsed time, we are not too exhausted and have not ruined our trip. (Just another reason to book your own flights via your travel agent.)

Coming back from Asia is a whole different ballgame! First you are dealing with the International Date Line and "repeating the day" in the process. Try to leave Asia in the evening, perhaps have a light meal and try to go to sleep. You will arrive on the West Coast during the day, and you can make your connection before total exhaustion sets in!

Travel to/from South America is also exhausting. Although the time changes are not as severe, it is still a ten-plus hour flight between the United States and Rio, Buenos Aires, or Santiago.

Obviously, the closer you live to the US embarkation city, the better. Perhaps a second flight will not be necessary. If this is the case, don't try to drive home. It is much safer to have a driver. While aboard your transoceanic flight, try to eat lightly, avoid heavy drinking, get up and stretch every hour or two, and try to sleep if you can. Such a self-disciplined regimen will serve you well during the following week at home.

Now you have gone, had a great time, and returned home safely and without calamity, it is time to get out the map—where shall we go *next*?

EPILOGUE

Writing this, my first book, has been an exciting adventure. I hadn't realized that we have been to so many places until I began to list them! This has really been a travel memoir, causing me to think back and remember where we went and what we did. I hope that you will find the book both educational and entertaining.

With this project behind me, I am now ready to hit the road. The book has helped me realize that there are a few places that are calling me for a return visit. I would now like to solidify those memories rather than build new ones—Paris, London, and Scandinavia come to mind. For years, business travel allowed me to visit all fifty US states. They are no longer on my bucket list.

If I have rekindled your interest to continue traveling, the writing of this book has been worthwhile. It has also documented, in many ways, the history of my life.

Should you have specific questions about the places mentioned, the opinions expressed, or general inquiries, feel free to contact me at *meicher@cox.net*.

On another, somewhat related topic, I happened to think that *writing a travel book* is a good way to create a legitimate tax deduction! Royalty payments to the author are well documented, as is the manuscript/book, the contract with the publisher, and the receipts garnered from the travel and related expenses of the author. *Too bad that I didn't think of that years ago when I began my travels!* Unfortunately, writing a *book* was not on my mind at that time.

ABOUT THE AUTHOR

Mike Eicher is in his mid-seventies and lives with his wife in Scottsdale, Arizona. They try to take two big trips each year, usually cruises. They have two daughters, living in Santa Fe and Chicago, who love to travel as well, often as a family. Throughout a marriage of more than fifty-two years, they have traveled the world on business, for pleasure, and as leaders of church pilgrimages. They have lived in California, New York, Miami, Honolulu, Indianapolis, St. Louis, and Toledo, Ohio, among others. As youngsters, both traveled with their parents. In high school, Mike was an exchange student, in Germany. Mike graduated with a B.S. degree in Hotel & Restaurant Administration from Cornell University, Ithaca, New York. For a number of years, Mike was CEO of several public companies; he also was president/CEO of the junior college system in the State of Indiana.

Since retiring, Mike has held political office, served on the town's planning and zoning commission (Carefree, Arizona), several corporate boards of directors, and written this book, his first effort as an author. In between it has been travel, travel, and more travel. He and his wife continued to travel, although slightly differently than before. To tell that story is the reason for this book. Mike hopes that other retirees who might think that they are now too old to travel, will think again and will also consider inviting their adult children or close friends/relatives to join them.

Odense Castle, near Copenhagen, Denmark

INDEX

Q

R

W

X, Y, Z